Time, and Times, and Half a Time

Wendy Mulhern

illustrated by
Susanna Maria Weiss

Earth Whispering Press
PO Box 598
Marcola, OR, 97454

wendymulhern.com

Copyright ©2021 Wendy Mulhern
Images Copyright ©2021 susanna maria weiss
All rights reserved.
isbn: 978-1-7361904-0-1

To Heather, forever beloved

For every parent who has lost a child

Contents

Mourning Song 8
Going through it 11
Transparent 12
Aquifer 15
Surrender 16
Mending 19
Lifting 21
Bright Release 23
Floods 24
Message from Heather 26
When we meet again 29
Between 30
Rooftop Prayers 33
Windows of Heaven 34
Time, and times, and half a time 37
A day with no name 39
Mother's Day 41
Deeper 42
Hush 44
Navigating 47
Sweeping down the centuries 48
Errands 50
Tree Therapy 53
My life now 54
Now you see it, now you don't 57
Continuing 59
As we move on 60
Progress Report 63
After the rain 64
Unconditional 66
Changes 69
The way forward 70

Cup and Puzzle	73
Answers	74
These Days	77
One Morning	78
Interim	81
Heather's Day	82
Old and New	85
Aftershock	86
My Life	89
Still talking to Heather	90
Here and Hereafter	93
Blessed are they that mourn …	94
Feathers	97
Our Days	99
Clear	100
The Nature of Now	103
As often as you need it	104
Demons Departing	106
Imagining	109
Under	110
Illusions of Refuge	112
Intersections	115
Even So	117
Huh	118
Walking in Truth	121
What does this mean?	122
To Heather	124
The Choir of Heaven	127
About this book	129
A Note from Heather's Dad	130
About the Author	136
About the Illustrator	137

Mourning Song

I have a bag of tears
somewhere in my head,
I feel it jiggle with the bumps
along the road,
maybe I'll take it out
and drink some down,
water my memories

Oh my sweetest love,
I miss you in my future,
I miss your presence, too.
The water comes
and takes away my footprints,
something like that sometime
may take me, too

I found a feather
amidst my sobs along the sand,
so small and perfect —
I smoothed it with my hand,
and as I always do
I had to take it for a sign
I had to listen
for your presence in my mind

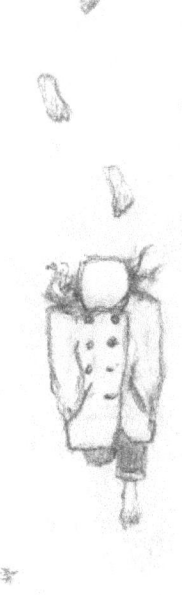

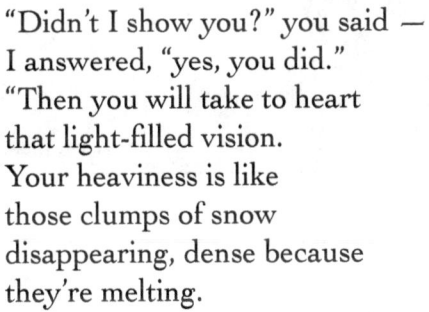

"Didn't I show you?" you said —
I answered, "yes, you did."
"Then you will take to heart
that light-filled vision.
Your heaviness is like
those clumps of snow
disappearing, dense because
they're melting.

"Take that feather
and learn to fly sometime,
get ready
to leave it all behind,
not that you're going anywhere,
just being redefined —
that's how I'll see you on the other side."

Going through it

wind driven rain
whips at the house,
rain falls through me
in waves, in recurring torrents

I'm like a spring tree,
my buds paused, my limbs wet,
water following its path
along my roots

I am not melting
though it may feel like it,
the soil will receive all of this —
my leaves will use it
to open out and grow.

Transparent

Well, I'm more transparent now,
it seems. Like I've part way come with you
into the place where these weights
just fall through me. And the constraints
of time and space and body
don't apply, at least as much

This state of me
is something I observe, and ponder,
and curiously feel what it's like
to be (at least somewhat)
unbound by physics,
to be caught up in different motivation,
to move like light through my day.

Aquifer

We will sit
in the comfort of each other,
we will talk
of things we know,
we will find solace
in the solidness of bodies,
in the quiet light
of shared confidences

There is a way forward —
it may come in settling back,
back into what feeds our life flow,
the shared aquifer of truth.

Surrender

I'll take what is given,
this storm, with roaring winds
and rain that slaps itself through screens
and runs down panes,
this sleep,

these people whose threads
are so deeply interwoven with my fabric
that we feel each other's tug,
each other's strength,

this truth, which settles out
(today, in luminescent teal)
so clear, so unassailable,
awaiting, but not demanding
my surrender, my return
to where I was before the world began.

Mending

Family folds us in
in ways we didn't know we could expect,
nets of connection bear us up,
many arms embrace us

So the mending begins,
of holes we mostly can't even see,
things that must be obvious to others —
places we are leaking,

Why we seem to need to keep sleeping,
simple tasks that seem impossible —
At some time we will have to rise up
and reassume our former mantles.
But for now we'll let ourselves be held
circled up in other people's care.

Lifting

Calmly we are instructed
to stop whatever it was we were doing,
whatever it was we were thinking,
and wait for the lifting,
the gentle sifting
where all the cold gray lumps
of worry, expectation, disappointment,
precipitate and fall away
and the pure joy
of flying in Soul's murmuration
becomes the center
of what and where we are.

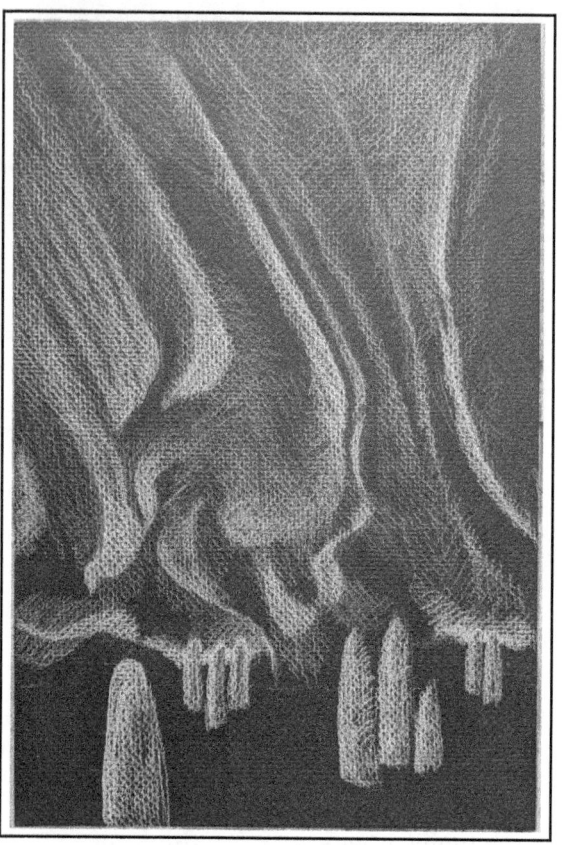

Bright Release

What will you do with this?
Mothers — take it, use it to love your children
even more than you have before,
Fathers, use it as a way
to deepen grace, to find your footing
in the place where your nobility
touches ground

Brothers, sisters, friends —
use this to remember
how tender and how tensile
is your connection to each other,
how paramount it is
to keep these ties
awake in your heart

All of you — take this bright gift,
this strong release of light,
this nourishment of life —
use it to celebrate
our common source
and the fountain of our days.

Floods

Every place we go back to, it seems,
presents another flood,
and surely it will cleanse us
and maybe it will drown us —
we can't know until we go there
and go through —
there is no other way out

So we will hold each other's hands,
we'll go together,
we'll be grateful for each sandbag
that kind people have thrown out
to shore us up, to lend support,
whether or not they feel they understand

We will go through —
who knows what
will be on the other side —
where we are now is all that we can know.

Message from Heather

Light rests on every life,
a gentle touch, a lifting breeze,
present reminder
of what makes our spirits rise

It shines amidst the bustle —
Whether noticed or ignored,
it is still there, and everyone
can feel it. Eventually, their inward light
will insist, and they will look up.

When we meet again

We know you will go on,
we know you will keep learning,
and we can consider
that you will share
your inspirations and your joys with us,
just as you did before

We will go on,
we will keep learning,
so we'll have things to share
next time we come together,
when we meet again.

Between

Alone, I find myself drifting
in some odd space
between hunger and tears.

The day is benign,
and everything is breathing —
Clearly, it all knows
that breath is gratitude,
and that it's enough
to fully engage with it,
taking in and releasing
in the dance of mutual blessing

It almost seems I could join with it.
It almost seems
like something I could never leave,
something I have never left.

Rooftop Prayers

Dust and pollen have sifted
through the quiet air,
the soft breezes,
warm and wistful,
have lifted
the scent of lilacs
and brought it here

I will reach through this
drifting afternoon,
to find the prayer
that knows the heart
of all these living things,
and brings me there,
where I, too, can know
my core and highest cause,
where I, too, can be the message
long awaited, gladly shared.

Windows of Heaven

"Prove me now herewith" —

For they are indeed open,
present in everything that fills with light,
waiting in the spaces
between our expectations

Windows of heaven
ready to pour forth such brightness,
such soul-gracing truth
that all our limitations dissolve.

We step across the threshold
caught up in glory.

Time, and times, and half a time

The heaping apple cart
tips over, the rolling hopes and expectations
jostle and fall,
bounce along roads,
lost to us now

We can't even begin
to gather them back,
and the cart is broken anyway,
one wheel following the apples down
careening and ringing like a coin

And it makes no sense to us
to go back, to start over —
What would it be to us, at this point?
So in the aftermath
we wait to be lifted,
our lives to be borne
along a different arc.

A day with no name

The day has stretched out long,
we have worked, we have prayed,
we have been busy, and also listless.

The sun is still splendid,
low through backyard trees
as the clock rolls past seven.

We will eat, we will cry,
we will clean up. A day
between the days,
a day with no name.

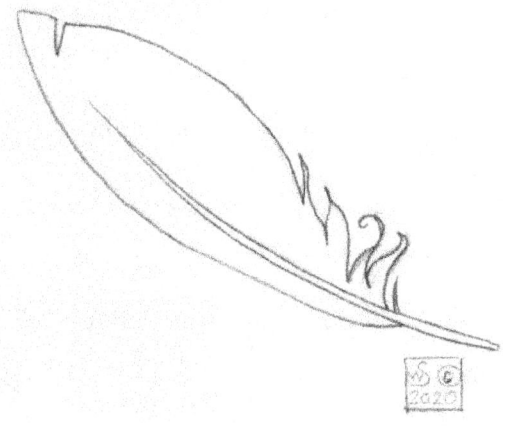

Mother's Day

A rose may be shared,
as also, perhaps, a child,
or at least, the ties of motherhood

This didn't come out as we expected,
did it, my love? But no matter —
it can be another thing we laugh about together

You, me, your dad, your brother —
we'll all have a good laugh at this,
next time we get together,
next time we take a walk along the beach.

Deeper

Beneath the pale etchings I have called my life,
something momentous moves,
something that fills out
more dimensions than I can count

Something so ultimately satisfying
that all I have attended to before —
all the inept scratchings,
all the lines I tried to set in place,
and what was scribbled over all my efforts
by other hapless hands —
amount to nothing

I settle myself
into the deeper motion
and am at peace.

Hush

This concentration of power
allows no excuses.
There is no weak spot in the field
where the potency could leak out,
could run away
There is no voice against it,
no answer to it.
We are hushed, aware
that nothing makes sense,
nothing gets a hearing
outside of this truth,
in the face of which
we lay our weapons
and our burdens down.

Navigating

We tried to go back to the old hills
but they were gone, tried to navigate
the once familiar paths,
but after walking them awhile
we could tell that we were blind
and couldn't see the markers

Strangely, we could also tell
that we had never seen them —
we had been content with blindness before —
now we can't abide it
and we would rather
not take any steps except
when walking in the light,
not say anything
unless we know it's true.

Sweeping down the centuries

Time is of no more use to me.
I've been forced to give it up.
From now on I will approach it broadsides,
I will move in the current
where our growing awareness of Spirit
sweeps up all the broken dreams of history,
sets to right every small and large sadness
that ever occurred,
unites us with our past and future generations
and chimes a chorus
that will echo throughout the vast eternity
where there is time no longer.

Errands

I walk these steps as if they were floes,
shifting under me like something
that sits on liquid —
I am surprised I don't feel more jostled
Something steadies me. Something like
light projecting my image over this surface,
so I'm never really needing
to catch my balance
Where I am exactly
is not clear to me, nor am I sure
of where I've ever been.
But it feels right to be here
and to keep walking.

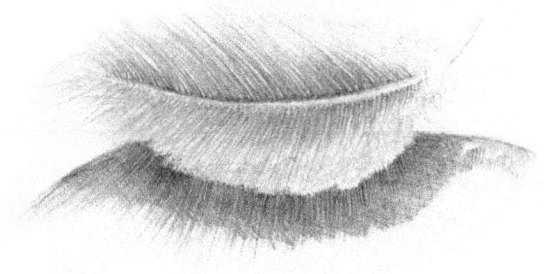

Tree Therapy

We walk hand in hand,
we look at trees in the park,
we feel the warmth of the sun.
Some things we don't need to talk about,
some things we do

I had a dream in the morning
where our girl came back to us
at any age she wanted, at any time.
I counted it for true
and I was happy,
but it didn't end the need to cry

There's much more to us
than the stories we could make about ourselves.
Every part needs to come along with us,
every part needs to be healed.

My life now

I learn the nature of myself
by what floats
and what sinks,
what opens up a grand expansiveness,
what traps me, lost, within its maze

I let each feeling have its say —
some leave me helpless,
some make me strong,
some will remain and some will pass away,
some are empowering,
none are wrong

I won't direct the process
but I will be sifted,
I will not save myself
but I will still be lifted,
I'll let the truth distill
the deeper gifts,
that shine the will to live,
that fill my life.

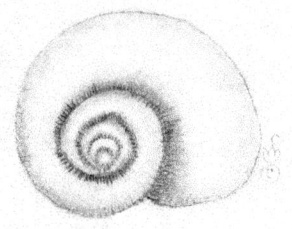

Now you see it, now you don't

It isn't that I've lost the will to live,
it's just that I'm so tired
of how I keep on running back
to the same old holes,
empty though they've always been —
keep on anticipating
that my thirst will finally be quenched

What does it take
to not be left again along the bank —
to ride the flow all the way down
to where I lose those habits
of seeking where there's nothing
and missing the deep healing of the day?

Continuing

And life asserts itself
unendingly, with patience and with joy,
in baby ducks and beavers
and herons on the wing
and that blackbird
with its exultant warble
in the late afternoon sun
that still reaches it, there in the treetop

Life continues, in dating and in weddings,
in friends confiding in each other,
in families, in passing generations

And we will, too,
affection being the most important thing —
we'll hold it tenderly
and we will rise.

As we move on

You will bring us joy every day,
long beyond the tears,
joy of presence, joy of spirit,
joy of every sweet thing
we learn from you

You still bring us
the hum of strong connection,
the swift running of emotion
and the sense of how important
all this is. Not schemes and plans
but simple daily being with each other,
you still teach us
every time we greet you in our hearts.

Progress Report

Baby steps toward healing —
being able to talk about it,
recognizing there was nothing
we could have changed,
given what we understood then,
given what we knew

Nothing that, had we done differently,
could have brought a different outcome.
Nothing short of
the salvation of the whole world
could make a difference

So there it is —
what could have helped us then
can help us even now.
We turn around and face the place
where dawn will come.

After the rain

These flowers bloom
even if their stems bow down,
even if their faces hit the soil
and their petals
begin to commune
with the ground, with the turning
of everything back
to the place of starting over,
humble and dark and untroubled
by being anything with a name,
anything but ready
for the things
whose time has come to begin.

Unconditional

I sense that I have barely comprehended
the size of unconditional
and what it means
to be companioned in that vastness,
comforted at every step

And how it is that there's no far away
in everpresence, no departure
from here. Space without distance,
development with no constraint of time,
nothing locked away by past or future,
everything at hand in earth and heaven.

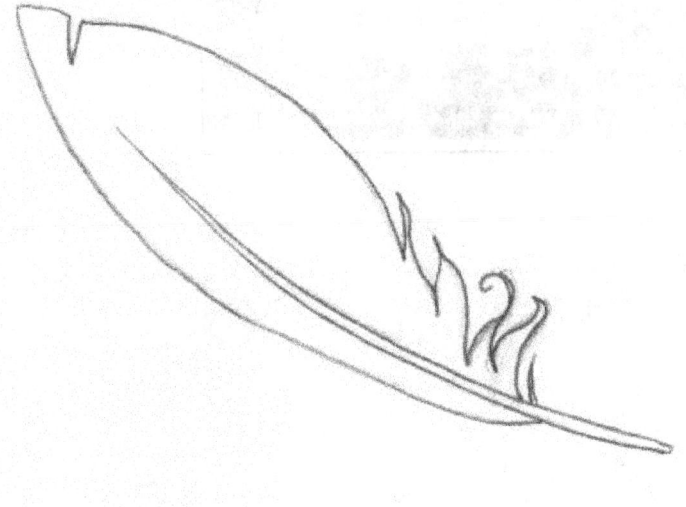

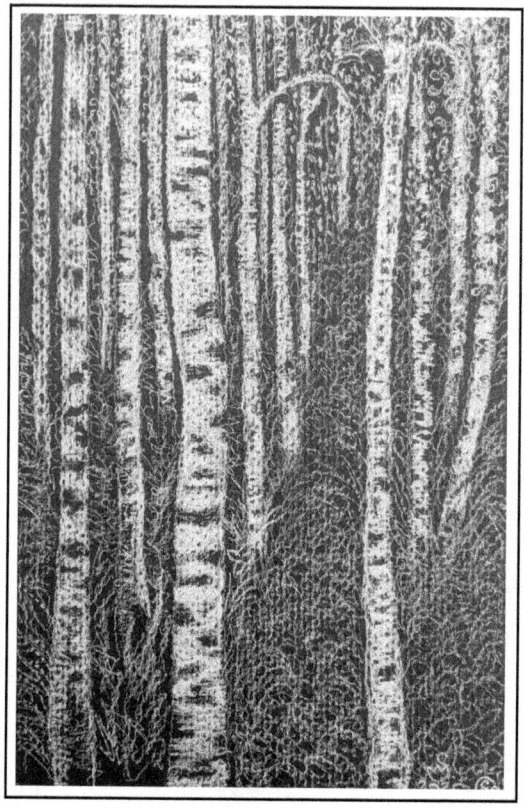

Changes

The only place we've ever lived
is in the place where we can never die.

This isn't what it looks like,
these days, these goals —
whatever I have thought of them before —
these changes . . .

Now I'll keep paying attention
to what lights us up
deep down at the source,
what makes us live and move
before we even enter all the surface fray

This isn't what it looks like
but it is something. Indeed,
it overrides whatever I had thought —
these changes, this which never changes.
This which I may find to be enough.

The way forward

In the way forward
there are no bragging rights,
no carefree membership
in some self-satisfied association

In the way forward
there will be solitude.
In the wilderness of
no one to ask for help
there is a hardening off, a honing,
a time of leanness
and a propelling hunger

Rumor has it
there is great reward on the other side,
that, upon arrival, there will be celebration,
singing. There will be that precious
everyday joy, as well as the special one
of having traversed the chasm

I don't know anyone here
who knows this from experience.
We shall see.

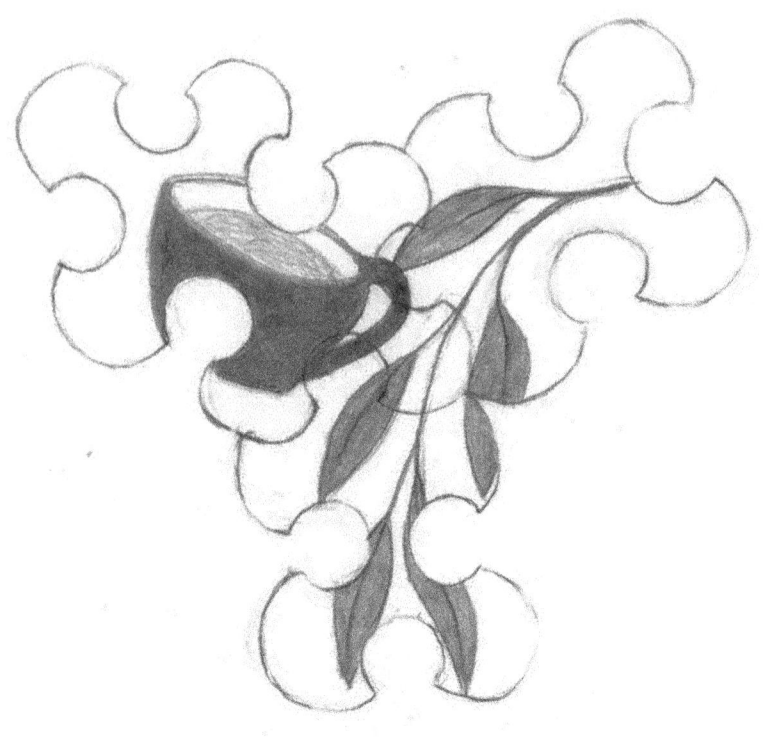

Cup and Puzzle

As to the question of
why I am here:
I am here for this moment,
here for this healing,
here for the cup of
whatever fills my day

The puzzle piece I am
is not improved
by trying to make it more
like other pieces
that have already fit in.
The puzzle piece you are,
likewise, will not be helped
by alteration

It is not mine
to choose another cup
but to drink this one
and be satisfied.

Answers

I ask myself the questions
but I don't know how it happens,
don't know how all these distant things
come together,
how we collect what we need,
how we join the pieces just right
so things really work

There are so many arenas
in which I don't know this answer

But I will note that,
in this one instance at least,
when I cried,
when I confessed my helplessness
(and after I had failed)
the answer came in
all by itself.

These Days

These days the bottom falls out of us
at unexpected times.

It could be a good thing,
dropping us through
our soggy cardboard efforts
to hold ourselves together,
down to the waiting, changing land,
the rain and all the spreading seeping
and the tender sparkles
of returning morning sun.

One Morning

One day you'll wake up feeling fine —
the dread that sullied
so many of your early mornings
gone — you'll feel, within,
the strong light rising,
pure as blackbird song

For this, this bright upwelling,
is what you're made of,
what you're made for, too.
The thin veneer on which anxiety is etched
must wear away,
leaving nothing but the true,
which overcomes,
which carries all the days.

Interim

There's a place for us at the table —
it's not the raucous one, at the center of things.
It's close enough to take in all the life
but far enough that we can move away
without a fuss, when we are done.

We circle, still, at the periphery,
and it feels good to be here
where we can observe but not be known,
where we can belong
but not be called upon.

Heather's Day

When I can remember
how time turns out to be
nothing at all,
how the wholeness of you
was complete before we knew you,
continued so, all throughout that span
and is so now,
then I can feel
the joy of your being
that touched so many moments
and blessed so many hearts
so thoroughly, then as now,
and I can know
a similar purpose
attends each of us.
Your light can still
guide us there.

Old and New

I can't walk easy
along the paths I used to walk,
hedged by familiarity,
bordered, more distantly, by fear.
I can't pursue the old hopes,
flanked by worry, with the protections
of bravado and blurred vision

I have to walk
now as ever
in the clear bright world
that has always been here, too —
a plain without paths,
a presence without arriving,
being caught up in the offering
of myself, like a mirror,
to the light.

Aftershock

Nobody knew the right thing to do.
Lots of people would have had stuff to say,
opinions on appropriate directions

Where was my intuition?
Why had I not been
honing it through many years?
How could I have thought
it was unreachable or optional?

If I had known better,
could I have done better?
If I had done better
where might we be?

This wave comes over me
and passes through
and in its ebb I feel again
how I was grounded.
There will be other waves —
when they recede
the light will gleam again
along the sheening sand.

My Life

My life is a shed skin.
I move, now, in a different being,
stretch and curl myself
with a vibrance not my own
in which I work daily
to hold without owning,
inhabit without habit,
affect without affect —
a being in which I labor
to be true to what is true.

Still talking to Heather

Here is a thing that is beautiful:
your life, and what it proved,
what it establishes, even now —
that no one ever has to think
their presence is expendable,
their friendship unneeded
or unwanted

You are here
with your ready hug
and your deep empathy,
and you have showed us
that no one needs to wait to love
and no one has to wait
to be beloved

So we go back
along the weaving of a life,
the places in the past
where strands have tangled,
we pick them up
and lay them back in place
gently and deftly,
as your hands always moved

We set things right
all along the years,
we feel in doing this
that you are here.

Here and Hereafter

You're looking for connection
in a cosmic sense,
like a lost lover in a story,
a lost father actually,
seeking his daughter
across oceans, across skies

It's archetypal
and it opens up the portals
into other worlds —
your longing has already
crossed the bridge
so you can't live easy here

Can't confine yourself,
have to accept that you've expanded,
have to learn to move and feel
in the world where she is,
must be reunited
in the larger sphere.

Blessed are they that mourn ...

I will not let thee go, except thou bless me

Before they sing, the little birds
expand to almost twice their size,
taking the morning in,
filling themselves up
with what will be their song
so it expresses
all the joy and glory that they feel

You will be like that,
so deeply filled with what has saved you
that comfort will pour forth like birdsong,
blessing everyone who hears.

Feathers

I hold you as a frame,
as branches frame a far off scene,
as a path frames the woods,
showing the exquisite composition
of the view
and turkeys, browsing every day
along that path, frame the afternoon

I see feathers. They fall from the sky
or are found, in delicate perfection,
along a road, beside the lake.
I take them as signs.
I think of you every day.

Our Days

We do what we can
in the aftermath of tears,
in the relentless beauty of days
and the work that is too much for us

We will go home again
tired to the bone, and weathered,
but also saturated in song —
tree song and cricket song
and the creaking flap of raven flight

We will return, as we have
so many times. We'll take up
the work we couldn't finish.
We'll struggle through the cold
of the long edges of days
and be graced by their brilliance,
and learn the meaning of work,
perhaps. And the meaning of praise.

Clear

Let me lay down the confusion
that has beset my years,
let me recognize
our lives were never about this

We are not tokens, moved along a board,
we are not pawns nor rooks nor queens
nor even players.
The realm we move in
has always been the infinite —
not mind within the body
but body in the mind —
our consciousness reveals
the size of what we are

It may be hard
to come to this life knowing,
and have the knowing steadily displaced.
We won't be always fooled,
we will shine clear,
and what we are will surface in our days.

The Nature of Now

This transformation
is like leaving the land,
stepping into the sea,
swimming into the depths offered,
former concerns forgotten

Let me grasp it
just in this little moment —
that will be enough.
I can stand on this moment
and ride out to eternity,
since that is, of course,
the nature of now.

As often as you need it

You were here
when the morning stars sang together,
you were here
at the foundation of the earth

When you know yourself as essence,
as what steps out in wonder
at the gifts of the day,
you can see that years
have never changed you,
and all the twists of circumstance
will always fail to knot you up
in some unfortunate condition

Your belovedness
is clear as light
and as immutable —
you don't need
to make yourself be anything —
you are here

And I will tell you this
every day, every hour,
as often as you need it,
and if I weren't here
the day would still
tell you the same thing.

The trees, the wind,
the bright waves on the water
—they will tell you,
and the birds will, too.
Listen, and you will hear.

Demons Departing

When demons are cast out,
they may go arguing with each other,
as they always do,
disputing their turf,
and which ones
have loftier positions

They may scream and whine and howl,
as they always do,
they may curl up
intending not to move

But they'll go anyway,
dissolving even as they speak,
their threats and bludgeons
dissolving with them.
They'll leave the field in blessed silence,
so clear that you can hear a dewdrop fall.

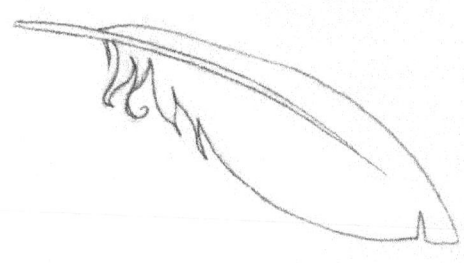

Imagining

I'm imagining us, not too long hence,
walking hand in hand
though in the vision
it's more like streaming light,
all of us grateful
to have been brought together

I imagine us streaming like that
all the time — then I consider
you will have others, too,
others to share and celebrate
and so will we
and the whole thing
will be so much grander
than I can think up

So I'll just bask in the warmth of it,
how it comforts me and holds me up
right here and now.

Under

We started to feel underwater
though it was just under rain —
under rain, and under tears,
under memories, and under
the warp of time

We tried to speak
but our words were garbled,
bubbles rising up,
purpose having floated off
somewhere else

We couldn't hold ourselves to anything,
couldn't stay grounded,
couldn't fly up to the surface for air

Our only hope
was to close our eyes for long enough
that when we opened them
the whole strange scene would be gone.

Illusions of Refuge

And if your refuge fails you
or if it says you've failed
and thus cannot avail yourself of safety

Or if your refuge
is put in question
by someone else's sense of truth

Or if the solace it provides
has grayed, has faded,
has been rendered hollow

Don't be afraid.
For even as your demons rage
and push you towards the center,
as the edges crumble
and your space grows smaller

You are already redeemed.
You were delivered
even before the dawning of your first day.
Your substance is secure,
your realm is infinite —
you need no refuge,
for you own your grace.

Intersections

We may walk together
along these paths,
along these stories,
we may share vistas
but this is not an open beach —
I am aware of holes
big enough to get lost in

Mostly
I'm not mentioning them,
I'm choosing ways
to go over or around them,
things I think you can believe,
things that won't demand you
to walk the miles with me
through and out of darkness,
things that won't demand you
to veer off wildly
from what you perceive.
Perhaps you also do the same for me

We only know each other
at the intersection of our known worlds,
and that's the sector we can walk together.

Even So

If every life story
turns out not to matter,
if none of the shocks and the falls
or the haunting doubts
or the lonely lows
can make any mark on your being

If none of your items of pride
with their giddy highs,
their sidelong looks
(weighing your relative worth)
are anything you can protect,
anything that can remain

Still you will find
that the spark of your love
and all you're compelled to defend,
your unplumbable worth
and the need for your presence
shine in Life's eyes without end.

Huh

Turns out, it seems,
I'm not afraid of death.

It is a subtle thing,
the lack of terror — no struggling up
of something held at bay,
no frantic pushing back
against the upflow,
no fear-frayed patches present in my prayer

A thing to only notice in thunderstorms
(bike tires plowing through the water,
lightening flashing, touching down ahead)
or in an airplane, when they talk about
the life vests,
or other times I haven't yet observed

Not that I have a death wish, either —
I'd rather have my life be affirmation
that Life is here, and kind,
I'd rather be here for the folks that count on me
but being unafraid —
that's something I don't mind.

Walking in Truth

Feet step out in wonder —
Try to describe this,
soaring down the tailwinds,
bright spirited day after the squall

Flowers bloomed where she walked —
that was one way to say it,
joy meeting joy

not something precious or singular,
just the natural way of moving
and its expected effects

Surely goodness and mercy
shall follow me
(I shall have a legacy of blessing)
all the days of my life

that's a way to say it, too,
in the house of presence
where each breath
brings forth fruit.

What does this mean?

What does this mean:
it's not too late? —
when life has rolled on down its path
and suddenly I wonder
why I didn't think to take a different course —
what it could have been
if I had better understood
and had availed myself
of current opportunities

If I had not been closed,
if I had recognized
there was another way
to think or act

What does it mean,
it's not too late?
I don't know what it means
but I am willing to believe,
willing to wait in wonder
to see how this can be true.

To Heather

My song sparrow, my thrush, my swallow,
May your sweet voice carry on the wind,
May you swoop in sheer delight
in concert with your kin

Since you took off, I've been trudging up this path,
Sometimes caught up in overwhelming beauty,
Often looking down and thinking it should be so easy
to just leap off and fly among these vistas

But I walk – there's plenty here,
and nothing else to do but keep on climbing –
One of these days I'll catch the peak
and then we'll see you maybe –
in that transfigured place where you have flown.

The Choir of Heaven

To bring in range the choir of heaven
consider what it means
that there be no more death —
not now or ever — that the whole veil
be drawn away, and we perceive that
no one, and nothing, has ever died

If there has been no loss
of loved ones, or of wisdom,
or of life experience,
of ancient ways of knowing,
of lessons dearly learned,
of birds and animals,
of fish, of trees,
of anyone who loved them

That whole choir of ancestors
and children, and newly resurrected hope
would fill the realm of home,
would fill infinity —
Yes, I will be there, too
and yes, I too will sing.

About this book

In 2018, my husband and I lost our daughter Heather, when she was 25. Two things happened to me at that time; one, the shattering of everything I called my life, in terms of meaning and purpose; and two, a great influx of spiritual sustenance along the lines that my daughter and I had been urgently searching since her first appearance of illness in 2015. I felt that she had received the answers we were seeking but I still had to pursue them.

My life since then has been fully devoted to that search and practice. Since my former sense of my life was gone, I felt I had no choice, nor any other desire. The spiritual sustenance that got me through the initial loss of my daughter has continued to feed me, continued to grow clearer.

The poems in this book are ones that I wrote during the first two years since Heather's passing. They reflect the grief, the efforts for healing, the difficult work of continuing with daily life, and the spiritual light that has powered my quest and sustained me through this difficult passage. My hope is that they can provide some light and comfort for others traversing this unchosen path.

A Note From Heather's Dad

Following the passing of our daughter Heather, it was not uncommon for people expressing condolence to say something like, "I can't imagine …" And, I would sadly think, 'yes, that is true, you can't imagine' – and prior to this horrible event that ripped through our lives, neither could I. Now, the feeling of unbridled joy is a stretch for me to imagine.

In losing Heather I lost an aspect of my self-identity: father of an exuberant, creative, self-confident, beautiful daughter. An honor I knew for many years.

My thoughts, my emotions, have been a tangle of confusion for the past several years. Wendy, more than anyone else, can relate to what I find so difficult to express openly. If she comes upon me when I am under water, I only need to say one word, 'Heather', and Wendy is immediately in tune with my grief in that moment. Wendy's poem, *Still Untold*, printed below, is her gift to me, to ease my pain.

Still Untold

You wanted to stand up and speak,
you wanted your story
to be told,
you wanted them all to know
how much she meant to you

But all your words kept being swallowed
in second guessing and regret,
and by the knowledge that your anguish
wasn't something you could convey, anyway,

*wasn't something that people
had the capacity to hear.*

February 14, 2021

Yesterday, Wendy asked me if I had been crying. She had heard me listening to a music recording of our son, Eric, performing *Sprinkle To Rain* at a High School event. He, a freshman then, had recently transcribed Isaac Shepard's original piano music for guitar. Heather, a senior, was an editor for the school's student creative arts magazine that produced the yearly event. While listening to the recording I had a clear visual memory of Heather proudly introducing the next performer, her brother. I very much appreciate the pride and caring that Heather held for her brother since his birth. I very much went to pieces while listening and remembering that evening.

I read the poems presented in this book, one at a time, as Wendy first penned them. It is important that Wendy was inspired to select these poems for this book. Only near the end of that process, when asked to give my editorial comment, did I have the courage to reread them. I say courage because reviewing them required my conscious focus on the specific circumstances underlying familiar murky waves of my grief.

It is bittersweet reading these poems, and I find that I can do it. And, in doing so I am choosing to release the hold that grief has on me. In doing so, will I no longer regret the difficult horrific events that my daughter endured, that I, her father, was unable to free her from?

At the very least I may come to accept what passed. Wendy's poems, *Surrender*, *Transparent*, and *As often as you need it* are, for me, guidance.

My emotion of grief and my desire for Heather's journey beyond the corporeal life/death divide are divergent. The grief is rooted in sadness for what might have been and what has passed (or at least the way it passed). Whereas, my desire is for Heather as bliss and freedom – freedom from physical constraints, and from need for the permission of someone or some agency for her to follow her spontaneity of passion and creativity. My desire is that Heather's passing (from a physical perspective) was a return to her full awareness of her spirit nature and sovereignty.

A Father's Appreciation and Gratitude

Heather's presence in this world was a gift to many people who had good fortune to know her. And, I know Heather was enriched by them as well. As Heather and Eric grew through childhood, many kids (and their parents too) frequented our home for parties and plain ole' everyday play. There are too many of you to list here. You know who you are – take a bow, you are appreciated. Through college and beyond, Heather moved across the country to another city and another group of friends from her school, work, and church. She appreciated you all. You were integral to her stepping into the fullness of her womanhood and spiritual identity. Thank you.

Heather was fortunate in receiving guidance and inspiration from her teachers from 1st grade through college. You all did good!

On the day of Heather's passing I was crazy with grief, regret, anger and urgency. A dear family friend responded to my middle of the night call for assistance and was at my door shortly before dawn to ferry me to the airport. Aud - Heather, Wendy and I love you.

Following Heather's passing, Wendy and I spent several surreal weeks camped out in Heather's last apartment. We were surrounded by Heather's belongings and creativity – ghosts of Heather having passed that way. Heather's roommates and friends cared for us and prepared a beautiful memorial for Heather. Through a veil of grief I somehow mustered enough focus to attend to Heather's funeral arrangements and oppressive legal and IRS matters of estate. Thank you to all of Heather's Boston area tribe.

Wendy, Eric, and I returned to Heather's grandmother's house with Heather's ashes. Near empty by then, I immediately sought out a family friend, Nat, for assistance. The next day we all returned Heather's remains to the Atlantic Ocean where she loved to sail when visiting her Grandmother. Nat and Pam, your gift of assistance was immeasurable. Heather felt the bow of Charlotte cutting the water surface, her last ride in a sailboat. All I have is deep gratitude.

On the west coast, close friends of Heather prepared a memorial for Heather's childhood community. Keira, Allie and Aud – thank you for making that happen. And, thank you to everyone else who participated.

And, of course Heather was gifted with all of her family through both Wendy and me. From her early childhood she was delighted to be associated with you all, to know that she had a secure seat at the family table. You are loved.

Susanna, your artwork for this book is a beautiful complement to Wendy's desire for the look and feel of the book. As a casual observer, I noticed and appreciated how smoothly and easily you and Wendy worked together. I appreciate your holding to getting it right, and that your artist's pencil can describe images in either minute detail or as a sweep of a gesture, as needed.

Earlier I stated that Wendy's publication of this book is important. It is important that Wendy's inspired and rich poetry be read more broadly – time to extend the audience reach. It is important to me that Wendy's poetry chronicling this grave passing be available. Reckoning with life and death is something germane to the human experience. She insists on seeing through tragedy to the light of spirit that twinkles just beyond. And, it may very well be important to you the reader. If you find value in reading this book, please drop a brief line of appreciation to Wendy. Her contact info is at the front of the book.

Edward Mulhern

About the Author

Wendy Mulhern is a poet. She writes a poem a day, and publishes her poems on her blog at wendymulhern.com, where you can also find information about her print publications. This is her 10th book of poetry.

She is now homesteading with her husband in Oregon. They lost their daughter, Heather, in 2018, when she was 25. Their son is a musician and renaissance thinker, living in Massachussetts.

About the Author

Wendy Mulhern is a poet. She writes a poem a day, and publishes her poems on her blog at wendymulhern.com, where you can also find information about her print publications. This is her 10th book of poetry.

She is now homesteading with her husband in Oregon. They lost their daughter, Heather, in 2018, when she was 25. Their son is a musician and renaissance thinker, living in Massachussetts.

About the Illustrator

Susanna Maria Weiss is an Artist, with all her heart.

A native of Germany, she first came to the US as an exchange student, but it was the magnificent beauty of the raw landscapes that brought her back several years later permanently, and eventually to her beloved Oregon. Besides being an illustrator, she is a painter and a sculptor. She finds her inspiration in close communication with nature, inviting Nature's beauty to reveal its essence and patterns to be captured on canvas, wood, paper or clay.

Her attraction to this publication of poems was both personal and spiritual. The poet and her husband are friends with the artist, and the artist had briefly met their daughter.

Contact the artist through her website: susanna-maria-artist.com

www.ingramcontent.com/pod-product-compliance
Lightning Source LLC
Chambersburg PA
CBHW051828160426
43209CB00040B/1979/J